CHRISTMAS:
RECEIVING & GIVING
LOVE

ANOTHER CHRISTMAS BELOVED!

Can you sense it in the air—cold weather, blistering winds, glistening snow, warm fireplaces, Handel's Messiah and the Carpenter's Christmas albums, pine needles and scented candles, the exciting "rush" of preparation: invitations, gifts to buy and wrap, special dinners to make?

Maybe Christmas won't be like this for you. Have you lost loved-ones to death or some other separation in this life—another Christmas and "They won't be coming!"? Perhaps you're facing your own health problems. Or maybe you're healthy but not fortunate enough to have that warm fireplace, dinner, and friends to share it all with.

There's hope beloved! A time is coming when "there will be no more pain or death or curse"; and there is a Gospel that tells us that not only is this true but also that no suffering in this life can outweigh it by comparison (2 Corinthians 4:16-18).

All this because of Jesus—"the 'Christ' in 'Christmas'!" Because these things are so, because pain is diminished by eternal hope and because it's dispensed with altogether by eternity, we've written this family study of God's Word to prepare your hearts for this Christmas. We're convinced the power of this eternal Gospel (Revelation 14:6) will lift your spirits out of any pain and misery you're experiencing. And if you're not hurting personally, you can share these truths with a friend or stranger who is.

This Study is based on Kay's 5-day Precepts For Life Program "Receiving and Giving Love." Kay's CDs and DVD are currently available on our EStore.

This Christmas, start a new tradition—prepare your family by soaking in God's Word together.

We sincerely hope and pray that you will enjoy these studies intended to draw you to the Father of Christmas and to His Son, the Lord Jesus, born on this day to be the Savior of the World . . . your Savior! May He create new faith in your heart this glorious season originally heralded by angels.

Visit precept.org/resource for more Free Bible Study Resources!

PRECEPTS FOR LIFE
with Kay Arthur
™

PRECEPTS FOR LIFE™
Study Guide

This Bible study material was designed for use with the TV and Radio teaching program, Precepts for Life™ with renowned Bible study teacher Kay Arthur, a production of Precept Ministries International. This inductive 30-minute daily Bible study program airs on many satellite, cable, and broadcast stations, and on the internet at **www.preceptsforlife.com.**

As with all Inductive Bible studies, the best way to use the material is to complete the assignments in each lesson before listening or watching the PFL program for that day. These programs are also available on DVD and CD at **www.preceptsforlife.com** or by phone (1.800.763.1990 for television viewers or 1.800.734.7707 for radio listeners). For more information about the Precept Inductive Bible Study Method and Precept Ministries International, visit **www.preceptsforlife.com.**

These materials are also useful for Bible study apart from the Precepts for Life™ programs. We hope you'll find them valuable for studying God's Word and that your walk will be strengthened by the life-changing Truth you'll encounter each day.

Christmas—Receiving and Giving Love STUDY GUIDE
Published by Precept Ministries of Reach Out, Inc.
P. O. Box 182218
Chattanooga, TN 37422

ISBN–13: 978-1-62119-484-2

All Scripture quotations, unless otherwise indicated, are taken from the *NEW AMERICAN STANDARD BIBLE*®(NASB) © Copyright 1960, 1962, 1963, 1968, 1971, 1972, 1973, 1975, 1977, 1995 by the Lockman Foundation. Used by permission. (www.lockman.org)

Printed in the United States of America

Precept, Precept Ministries International, Precept Ministries International the Inductive Bible Study People, the Plumb Bob design, Precept Upon Precept, In & Out, Sweeter than Chocolate!, Cookies on the Lower Shelf, Precepts For Life, Precepts From God's Word and Transform Student Ministries are trademarks of Precept Ministries International.

PROGRAM 1 — Receiving and Giving the Gift of Christmas Love

TODAY'S TEXTS
Ephesians 3:14-19; 1:3-5
John 3:16
Galatians 4:4-5
Matthew 20:28
John 1:1-3, 14
Romans 8:28-32

CROSS-REFERENCES
Matthew 12:50
Ephesians 1:4
Romans 8:35, 38-39

1. Read Ephesians 3:14-19 marking *Father* including pronouns with a purple triangle, *family* with a green box and *love* with a red heart.

   a. Where do *families* exist according to the text?

   b. Who are they named after? Are "all the saints" (v. 18) a family? (See Matthew 12:50.)

   c. Briefly summarize things Paul prays that God will grant "us" . . .

2. Read **Ephesians 1:3-5** underlining *chose* in red, boxing *in Christ* and *in Him* in red, and marking *love* with a red heart.

   a. When did God choose "us"?

   b. For what purpose did He choose us?

   c. Are you **"in"** Jesus Christ? Have you received His gift of eternal life?

3. Read **John 3:16** and mark *God* and pronouns with a purple triangle and *loved* with a red heart.

   a. Who did God give, who did He give it to, and what do they get?

   b. Why did God give this gift?

4. Observe **Galatians 4:4-5** again marking *God* and pronouns as above.

   a. When did God send His Son forth?

   b. What was His purpose? That we might receive _____

5. Observe **Romans 8:28-32**. Again mark *God* and pronouns as above.

   a. How are "the called" defined with respect to God—those who what?

   b. What did God predestine them to?

| PROGRAM 2 | **Receiving the Gift of God's Love** |

TODAY'S TEXT

John 15:13

Matthew 1:18-21

1 John 4:7-12

Matthew 1:21-23

Galatians 3:13-14

Matthew 27:26-29

CROSS REFERENCES

John 3:16, 17; 13:2-4

Hebrews 10:7

Galatians 4:4, 5

1 John 2:2

Matthew 20:28

John 10:10

1. Read John 15:13 and mark *greater love* with a red heart.

   a. From all the way back to John 13:2-4, where was Jesus when He said these things?

   b. How does He define *the greatest love* and what does this have to do with where He's going . . . and Christmas . . . and you?

2. Now read Matthew 1:18-21. Mark *Holy Spirit* with a purple triangle and underline *for*.

   a. How was Jesus conceived?

   b. What "disgrace" (shame) did Joseph want to save Mary from?

3. Read 1 John 4:7-12 marking *love* with a red heart.

   a. Why should believers love one another according to verse 7?

   b. What's the connection between believers' love for each other, the new birth, and knowing God?

   c. While God *does* love, what more do we learn about Him from v. 8?

4. Review Matthew 1:21-23 and mark *Immanuel* with a purple cross and underline shaded yellow.

   a. What does this name mean?

   b. Can you find the Old Testament reference?

5. Read Galatians 3:13-14 marking *curse* with an orange cloud shaded brown. What did Jesus *do* for us and *how*?

PROGRAM 3 | Giving the Gift of Love

TODAY'S TEXTS
John 14:1-3, 19-24
1 John 3:11-16
John 15:9-12; 14:31

CROSS-REFERENCES
1 John 5:11
John 3:16, 17
Matthew 25:32-46

1. Read John 14:1-3.

   a. Where is Jesus going?

   b. What is He going to do there?

   c. What will He do for us, His family, when He returns?

2. Now observe John 14:19-24 circling the "in" phrases and marking *love* with a red heart.

   a. How do believers "see" Jesus when the rest of the world does not? Is this the physical sight the world demands for proof? How does truth relate to this "sight"?

   b. How does Jesus characterize those who love Him (v. 21)? Is obedience something they should do, something they *actually* do, or *both*?

   c. How does Jesus characterize the one who does not love Him (v. 24)?

3. Now observe 1 John 3:11-16 again marking *love* with a red heart

   a. What is the message Jesus' followers hear "from the beginning"?

   b. According to v. 12, why do some people murder others?

   c. What does love for "the brethren" prove? Does this correlate with assurance of salvation? How can we be assured we're saved?

   d. What does hatred of a brother prove? Do "haters" have eternal life?

4. Now let's wrap up by observing John 15:9-12 and 14:31 again marking our two loves.

   a. How can we "abide" in Jesus' love? What do we have to do?

   b. What is Jesus' commandment?

| PROGRAM 4 | Giving And Expressing God's Love |

TODAY'S TEXT
John 15:9-19; 13:33-34

CROSS REFERENCES
John 3:16
1 John 4:9, 19-21
John 13:19, 34
John 14:21-23
Leviticus 19:18
John 15:13
Galatians 2:20
Romans 5:5

1. Read John 15:9-20 marking *love* with a red heart, *hate* with a red heart and a slanted black line through it, and _**abide**_ with an underline.

    a. How does Jesus love us?

    b. According to John 3:16 what action is connected with love? (See **Cross-reference** 1 John 4:9.)

    c. How do we abide in Jesus' love?

    d. Is love a form of obedience (v. 12, also **Cross-references** John 14:21-23 and 1 John 4:19-21)?

    e. What does Jesus call those who love and obey Him according to vv. 14-15? What does He call those who do not? In what ways do they differ?

    f. According to v. 15, what major gift do Jesus' friends receive from Him that outsiders do not?

    g. What else has Jesus done and what else does He do for His friends per v. 16? (See **Cross-references** John 15:13 and John 13:19.)

    h. How does the world's hatred for Jesus' followers "flesh out" according to vv. 20-21? What can we expect from the world?

2. Now read John 13:33-34 and **Cross-references** Leviticus 19:18, John 15:13, Galatians 2:20, and Romans 5:5. Mark *love* with a red heart.

    a. What is Jesus' "new commandment"?

    b. According to John 15:13, what is the *greatest* love?

    c. According to Galatians 2:20, who lives in believers? What do you think Paul means when he says "It is no longer I who live"?

    d. According to Romans 5:5, do we generate love by ourselves? Who or what helps us?

PROGRAM 5 — Dealing with Difficult Relationships

TODAY'S TEXT

Ephesians 4:1-2; 5:1-2

1 Corinthians 13:1-8

Ephesians 4:31-32

CROSS REFERENCES

Luke 23:34

Galatians 5:19-23

2 Peter 1:8

1. Read Ephesians 4:1-2 and 5:1-2 shading in purple every quality the Lord calls us to have.

   a. List the first four qualities "worthy of the [Lord's] calling" Paul mentions. See if you can find scriptures that define them and list the verses to the right.

   _____

   _____

   _____

   _____

   b. Who should we imitate and in what manner according to Ephesians 5:1-2? Specifically, what kind of love should we give to others?

2. Read **Cross-reference** Luke 23:34. How did Jesus respond to the worst provocation He endured?

3. Now read 1 Corinthians 13:1-8 shading in purple every quality of love.

   a. Verses 1-2: what can a person have and yet *not have love?* Can a person have "all faith" and no love? What does Paul say such a person is?

   b. Verse 4: How does each quality of love help us relate to "difficult" people . . . and other people both difficult and nice to relate to us? Think of examples. (See Ephesians 4:2.)

   c. Verse 5: What three things does love *not* do? What does "unbecoming" mean? Does the Word define "becoming" and "unbecoming" or does culture, or do both? See what you can find in the Bible.

   d. Verse 6: what does love *rejoice in* and *not rejoice in?*

4. Now read Ephesians 4:31-32 shading qualities we should "put away" in red and "put on" in purple.

   a. What are we to "put away" (v. 31)? _____, _____, _____,

   _____ and _____ . . . with all _____.

   b. What opposite qualities should we "put on"?

DISCOVER TRUTH FOR YOURSELF

Our passion is for you to discover Truth for yourself through Inductive Bible Study—a unique Bible study method you'll discover in the following pages and use throughout this study, as we engage this important topic together verse by verse.

You can't do a better thing than sit at Jesus' feet, listening to His every word. God's Word, the Bible, has answers for every situation you'll face in life. Listen to what God is saying to you, face-to-face, with truth to transform your life!

INDUCTIVE BIBLE STUDY METHOD

To study and understand God's Word, we use the Inductive Bible Study Method at Precept Ministries International. The Bible is our main source of truth. Before looking for insights from people and commentaries *about* the Bible, we get into the Word of God, beginning with observing the text.

❶ Observation

This is a very interactive process, well worth the time because the truths you discover for yourself will be accurate and profound. It begins by asking the five W and H questions.

Who is speaking? Who is this about? Who are the main characters? And to whom is the speaker speaking?

What subjects and/or events are covered in the chapter? What do you learn about the people, the events, and the teachings from the text? What instructions are given?

When did or will the events recorded occur?

Where did or will this happen? Where was it said?

Why is something said? Why will an event occur? Why this time, person, and/or place?

How will it happen? How will it be done? How is it illustrated?

Careful observation leads to interpretation—discovering what the text means.

❷ Interpretation

The more you observe, the greater you'll understand God's Word. Since Scripture is the best interpreter of Scripture, you and I will be looking at contexts and cross-references to enhance our understanding of the meaning of God's message.

Where should observation and interpretation lead? Application.

❸ Application

After we've observed the text and discovered what it means, we need to think and live accordingly. The result is a transformed life—the more you and I are in the Word of God and adjusting our thinking and behavior to its precepts for life, the more we are changed into the likeness of Jesus Christ! He is the living Word of God who became flesh, the Savior of the world, our coming King of kings!

SO WHERE DO YOU BEGIN?

The Bible is *God's* book, His Word, so when you study it you need to seek the Author's help. Begin with prayer, asking God to lead you into all truth, then open the Study Companion. (We suggest you work one program ahead of the broadcast to get the most out of the study.) Look at the general layout of each day's program and you will find the following:

- Introduction—usually with a challenging question
- Questions that contain pointers on using the Inductive Bible Study Method
- **Where's That Verse?** section containing the Primary Study Passage and several cross-references related to the topic
- Concluding Prayer

WHAT'S NEXT?

- In some programs, I'll point out key words to mark. You'll find many of them on the back cover of this Study Companion with *suggested* colors and symbols to spot them quickly in the text. Color coding key words helps you identify and recall. We have included a cutout bookmark so you can remember to mark each key word the same way throughout the text.

  You can mark these key words before or after the program, whichever is easier. You can also get the CD or DVD of the program and mark the key words later while studying.

Feel free to mark them your own way—there's nothing sacred about the particular symbols and colors I use!

- The cross-references I mention in these programs are under **Where's That Verse?** After you read them, you can jot them in the margins of the **Observation Worksheets** or write them in the wide margins of your Bible. I suggest you first pencil them in, then write them in ink later.

- For book studies, you'll find an **At A Glance** chart in the back. After we complete a chapter, record a summary theme there and in the space provided in your **Observation Worksheets**. Themes help you remember main ideas of chapters **At A Glance** after you finish the study. You'll also find these charts after each book in the *New Inductive Study Bible*.

MISSED A PROGRAM?

- Go to our website at **www.PreceptsForLife.com**. TV viewers can call 1.800.763.1990 and radio listeners 1.888.734.7707 to learn how to find programs online.

GETTING THE MOST FROM THIS STUDY

- Try to stay one program ahead of me so you'll learn directly from the Word of God and our time together will be like a "discussion group," as we reason together through the Scriptures. You'll get much more out of our time together if you've done this preparation.

- Try to memorize a key verse for every program covered. God will bring these to your remembrance when you need them!

- Pray about what you learn each day. Ask God to remind you of these truths and give you another person to share them with. These two exercises will do amazing things in your life.

- Get the CD or DVD set of this series and listen when you get ready for work in the morning, do chores around the house, or have family devotions. Or listen with an open Bible and discuss the teaching and its application to your life. Get together with a friend, view or listen to a message, and discuss it or use it for family devotions. You can also view or listen programs online. Visit **www.PreceptsForLife.com.**

- Request Precept's mailings to stay abreast of what God is doing around the world and to pray for the needs we share with you. You can be a significant part of this unique global ministry God is using to establish people in His Word. Here are some items you can request:

✦ The *Plumbline*—Precept Ministry's monthly e-newsletter that keeps you up to date on Bible study topics, products and events that help you in your walk with Christ.

✦ A prayer list so you can partner with us in prayer for our ministries in nearly 180 countries and 70 languages.

✦ "Inside information" each month when you join our "E-Team" of regular prayer and financial supporters. Visit **www.PreceptsForLife.com** for more information on how you can support our programs. (You can check out the current monthly letter right now on our website.)

✦ Advance notice of conferences at our headquarters in Chattanooga and throughout the United States and Canada.

✦ Information about our study tours in Israel and Jordan, where we teach various books of the Bible right where the action occurred!

• We use one of the most accurate translations of the Bible, the New American Standard (Updated). If the topic is a book study, our **Observation Worksheets** will contain the complete text. Since you'll be instructed to mark words and phrases and make notes in the text, you'll want to have colored pencils or pens available. As you grow in inductive study skills, you may want to use your Bible instead. We believe the best Bible to use is the *New Inductive Study Bible.* See our back pages to find out more about this ultimate study Bible. Now get started!

• Finally, stay in touch with me personally. I'd so love to hear from you by email or letter so I can be sensitive to where you are and what you're experiencing—problems you're wrestling with, questions you have, etc. This will help me teach more effectively and personally. Just email us at info@precept.org. (Don't worry, Beloved, I won't mention you by name; but as you listen, you'll know I've heard you!)

I'm committed to you . . . because of Him. The purpose of the "Precepts For Life" TV & Radio programs is to help you realize your full potential in God, so you can become the exemplary believer God intends you to be…studying the Bible inductively, viewing the world biblically, making disciples intentionally, and serving the Church faithfully in the power of the Holy Spirit."

That's my vision for us as believers! Won't you help us spread it to others?

Looking for people…looking for truth!

How Do I Start Studying The Bible?

Do you wonder,
God, how can I obey You and study your Word? Where do I begin? How can I discover truth for myself?

DISCOVER TRUTH FOR YOURSELF

There are some study tools we would recommend for you to begin with, as each will teach you the inductive method of study. By inductive we mean that you can go straight to the Word of God and discover truth for yourself, so you can say … "for You, Yourself have taught me" (Psalm 119:102).

Let's Get Started! For a jump start on inductive study, we recommend the following:

- *Lord, Teach Me To Study The Bible in 28 Days.* In this hands-on introduction to the basics of inductive study, you'll see why you need to study God's Word and how to dig into the truths of a book of the Bible. The instructions will walk you through the books of Jonah and Jude, and you'll be awed at what you see on your own! Discussion questions are included.

- *God, Are You There? Do You Care? Do You Know About Me?* This 13-week, self-contained inductive study on the Gospel of John is powerful and life-changing. Study the book of John, as you learn and put into practice inductive study skills. The Gospel of John was written that you might believe that Jesus is the Son of God and that believing, might have life in His name. You will know you are loved! Discussion questions are included.

- *How to Study Old Testament History and Prophecy Workshop.* Discover truths about who God is and how He works as you learn to study inductively, step by step, and be challenged to apply these truths to your life. This workshop will give you the tools to study and understand Old Testament history and prophecy. Go to www.precept.org or call 800-763-8280 to find out about workshops in your area, or online training.

- *How to Study a New Testament Letter Workshop.* Grow in the knowledge of the Lord Jesus Christ and His plan for your life. This inductive study workshop will equip you to study the New Testament letters and apply their truths to your life. Go to www.precept. org or call 800-763-8280 to find out about workshops in your area, or online training.

Now that you've begun . . . continue studying inductively using one of these:

- *40 Minute Bible Studies.* These 6-week topical studies are a good for personal study and a great way to start discipling others one-on-one or in a group setting—teaching them who God is, introducing them to Jesus Christ, and helping them learn God's precepts for life. These studies enable you to discover what God says about different issues of life. No homework is necessary for the students prior to group time.

- *The New Inductive Study Series,* now complete covering every book of the Bible, was created to help you discover truth for yourself and go deeper into God's precepts, promises and purposes. This powerful series is ideal for personal study, small groups, Sunday school classes, family devotions, and discipling others. Containing 13-week long studies, the New Inductive Study Series also provides easy planning for church curriculum! You can now survey the entire Bible

- *Lord Series.* These life-changing devotional studies cover in greater depth major issues of our relationship with God and with others, teaching us how to practically live out our faith. Ideal for small groups, these contain discussion guides and teaching DVDs are available for some.

- *Discover 4 Yourself®* is a dynamic series of inductive studies for children. Children who can read learn how to discover truth for themselves through the life-impacting skills of observation, interpretation, and application. You'll be amazed at the change that comes when children know for themselves what the Word of God says! Teach them now so they can stand firm in a first-hand knowledge of truth as they hit their teen years. This award-winning series is popular in Christian schools and among homeschoolers. Teacher's guides are available online.

- *The New Inductive Study Bible (NISB)* is a unique and exciting! Most study Bibles give you someone else's interpretation of the text. The NISB doesn't tell you what to believe, rather it helps you discover truth for yourself by showing you how to study inductively and providing instructions, study helps, and application questions for each book of the Bible, as well as wide margins for your notes. It's filled with many wonderful features that will guide you toward the joy of discovering the truths of God's Word for yourself. This Bible is your legacy.

GO DEEPER WITH OTHERS...
IN SMALL GROUP BIBLE STUDIES

Join others in the study of God's Word, sharing insights from the Scripture and discussing application to your life. Each of the studies described above are appropriate for groups as well as for individual study.

Discussion questions are included, so that you can dialogue about what you're learning with a group. These studies will teach you what it means to live by God's Word—and how it is applied to life. Learn about and discuss with others the truth that sets you free! To find out about inductive Bible study groups in your area, go to www.precept.org or call 800-763-8280.

DISCIPLE

How can you help others study God's Word inductively? Use the studies described above to share with others—one-on-one or in a small group. Lead others in discovering truth for themselves and experience the joy of seeing God change lives!

If you want training in how to lead these and other Precept Upon Precept studies go to www.precept.org or call us at 800-763-8280.

Precept Ministries International | P.O. Box 182218 | Chattanooga, TN 37422
800.763.8280 | www.precept.org

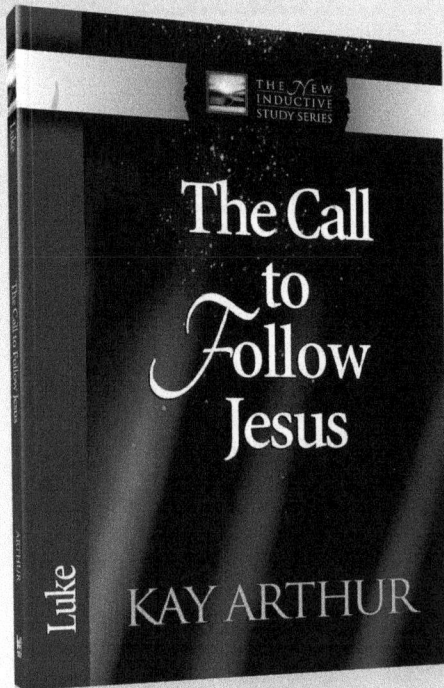

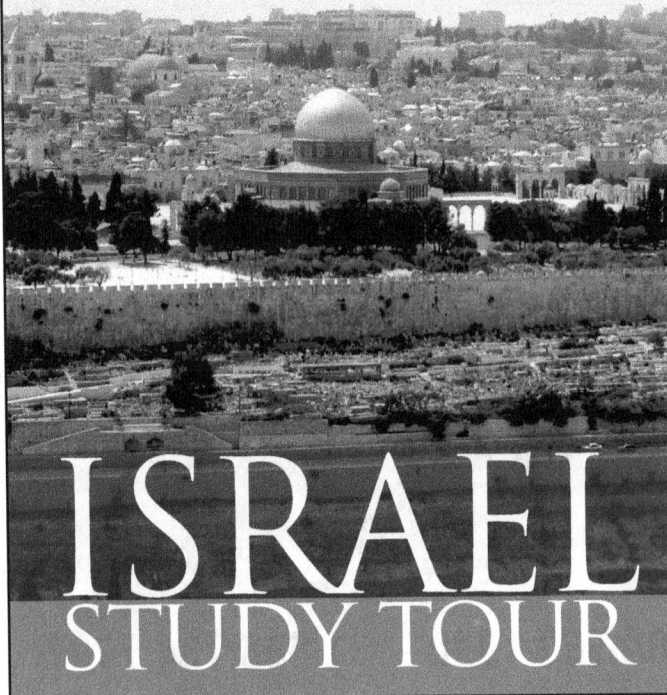

©2008 Precept Ministries International

14

Let us hear from you!

Have you been blessed by the teachings on *Precepts For Life*™? We'd love to hear your story.

Visit www.PreceptsForLife.com and click "Contact Us." Or write to:

Precepts For Life
P. O. Box 182218
Chattanooga, TN 37422.

Make sure to mention the call letters of the station where you tune in.

Did you know...

you can watch or listen to *Precepts For Life*™ whenever you wish? You can even download the programs to build your Bible study library or share with a friend.

Visit www.PreceptsForLife.com to study online—on your time.

www.ingramcontent.com/pod-product-compliance
Lightning Source LLC
Chambersburg PA
CBHW081238020426
42331CB00012B/3220